A New True Book

AIRPLANES

By David Petersen

*This "true book" was prepared
under the direction of
Illa Podendorf,
formerly with the Laboratory School,
University of Chicago*

CHILDRENS PRESS, CHICAGO

PHOTO CREDITS

Federal Aviation Administration, Great Lakes Public Affairs
Office—11, 17, 22 (lower left), 35, 39, 41, 44 (2 photos)
Department of the Army, Public Information Division—22 (top)
Cosette Winter—25
Art Thoma—2
NASA—45
Historical Pictures Service, Inc.—4 (2 photos), 6 (2 photos)
United States Dept. of Agriculture—32 (top)
Tony Freeman—Cover, 9, 22 (lower right), 27 (right)

Bellanca Aircraft Corp.—10   Gates Learjet—19, 43
Midway Airlines—37   U.S. Air Force photos—20 (2 photos)
James P. Rowan—13   Aerosport, Inc.—27 (left)
Smithsonian Institution—14 (2 photos)   Piper Aircraft Corp.—28
McDonnell Douglas Aircraft Corp.—16, 30   Lockheed Aircraft Corp.—32 (bottom)
Air France—18   Cover-Crop dusting

Library of Congress Cataloging in Publication Data

Petersen, David.
   Airplanes.

   (A New true book)
   SUMMARY: A basic introduction to many kinds
of airplanes and some of the jobs they do.
   1.   Airplanes—Juvenile literature.   [1.   Air-
planes]   I.   Title.
TL547.P39   629.133′34   81-7671
ISBN 0-516-01606-7   AACR2

TABLE OF CONTENTS

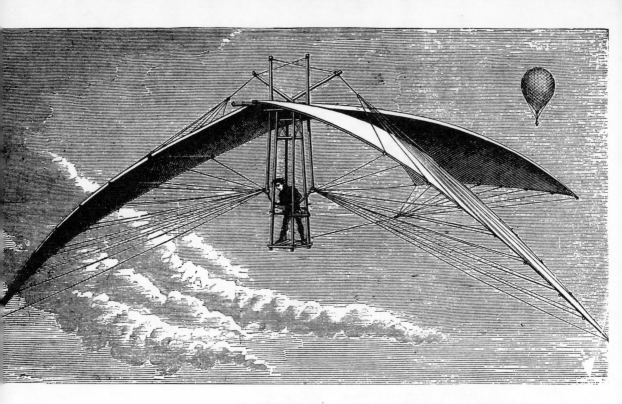

Above: Letarr's flying
machine, drawn
in 1883

Right: Otto Lilienthal's
glider, 1896

4

PEOPLE WANT TO FLY

Since the first human saw the first flying bird, people have wanted to fly.

People put on wings made of paper and wax. They built giant kites. They tied birds' feathers on themselves.

But nothing worked. People thought they would never be able to fly.

The Wright Brothers first tried their *Flyer* on
December 14, 1903 (above). They finally got it
to fly on December 17, 1903 (below).

Then, in 1903, two
brothers changed all that.
Wilbur and Orville Wright
built the first airplane that
worked. They called it the
Wright *Flyer*.

Orville Wright flew the *Flyer* 120 feet. This took only 12 seconds. It wasn't much of a flight—but now man had caught up with the birds!

It took people thousands and thousands of years to learn to fly. But in the next 70 years, people learned much more about flying. They learned so much that they made machines to send people to the moon!

HOW AIRPLANES FLY

Birds don't weigh very much. It is easy for them to fly. They have large wings to hold them up. A bird flaps its wings up and down. This gives it the power to fly.

In some ways airplanes are like birds. Airplanes also have large wings to hold them up.

But airplanes weigh a lot. They can't flap their wings like birds. Instead, they have engines. Engines give them the power to fly.

The engine makes power
to turn propellers.
Propellers are like big fan
blades. They spin around
very fast and pull the
airplane along.

Some airplanes can fly
without propellers. These
airplanes are called jets.
Jets have a different
kind of engine. A jet
engine pulls air into itself.
Then the air rushes out the
back of the jet engine.
This pushes the airplane
along. Jets can fly higher
and faster than airplanes
with propellers.

The Blue Angels jet team

Some jets can fly faster
than a sound can go.
Sounds go through air at
about 740 miles per hour.
If a jet can go faster than
that, we say it is breaking
the sound barrier.

The Bell X-1

The X-15

In 1947 an airplane called the Bell X-1 was flown. It was the first airplane to break the sound barrier.

In 1967 another airplane was tested. It was called the X-15. The X-15 went 4,534 miles per hour! That is about six times faster than a sound can travel.

Today many airplanes can fly even faster.

A DC-10 is a large airliner.

MANY KINDS
OF AIRPLANES

There are many kinds of
airplanes. Some are very
small. Some are large
enough to carry about 400
people.

16

Large airplanes that carry people are called airliners. One kind of airliner is the Boeing 747. A 747 has four jet engines. These push it along at 600 miles per hour. It can fly as high as seven miles up.

A 747

The Concorde, a Super Sonic Transport

Another large airliner is the Super Sonic Transport, or SST. The SST is the fastest airliner in the world. It moves at 1,400 miles per hour. SSTs also fly very high. They can go 60,000 feet above the ground.

There are also many smaller jets. One is the Lear jet. A Lear jet can carry six or eight people. It can go 500 miles per hour, and as high as 45,000 feet.

A Lear jet

F-105 fighters get fuel in the air

A B-52G bomber

The military uses many airplanes.

There are small jets called fighters. Jet fighters fly very fast. They can chase other fast planes. Some fighters are flown by just one person. Other fighters are harder to fly. They need two people.

There are large jets called bombers. They carry bombs.

Helicopters can lift
heavy objects.

Helicopters are special.
They can fly up, down,
forward, and backward.
They can land almost
anywhere. This makes
them good for jobs that
regular airplanes can't do.

A few airplanes can also
take off straight up. This
kind of airplane is called a
VTOL. That stands for
Vertical Take Off and
Landing.

HOMEBUILT AIRPLANES

Some people build their own airplanes. These are called homebuilt or experimental airplanes. Most homebuilt airplanes are very small. Many have room for only one person. Some have no roof. This is an open-cockpit plane. The pilot must wear goggles to protect his eyes.

An ultra-light experimental aircraft with a motor

One kind of experimental airplane is solar powered. A solar airplane uses the sun's light to make power for a small engine. This engine turns the airplane's propeller so it can fly.

AIRPLANES
WITHOUT ENGINES

Some airplanes have no engines. They are called gliders or sailplanes. Flying these airplanes is a sport. It is called soaring.

Another airplane or car must tow a glider up into the air. When the glider is high enough, its pilot lets go of the tow. Then the glider can sail around in

the sky for hours. It rides
on the wind made by
warm, rising air.

Other kinds of gliders
are called hang gliders.
Hang gliders are like large
kites. The pilot hangs
below the hang glider. He
turns it and steers it with
his body.

Left: Sailplanes in the air.
Below: Hang glider. Learning to fly a hang
    glider can be dangerous. The pilot
    jumps off a high hill to get going!

AIRPLANES
FROM YEARS AGO

Some airplanes were first
built many years ago. But
they are such good
airplanes that they are still
used today.

A Piper Cub

One of these airplanes is the Piper Cub. The first Piper Cub was built in 1930. It is slow. It flies only 87 miles per hour. But it is very safe. People often use Piper Cubs on ranches and farms. They are easy to land.

A DC-3

The DC-3 was the first airplane widely used as an airliner. It can carry 21 people. It can fly 180 miles per hour. Many businesses still use DC-3s.

JOBS AIRPLANES DO

Airplanes are used for many different purposes.

Some airplanes are used for fighting wars. Others are used to help people. Some airplanes carry both people and goods.

Large airliners carry passengers all over the world. So do smaller, private airplanes.

Some airplanes dust crops to keep
harmful insects away.

Mail is moved by plane. Here an entire post office for a far-away town in
Alaska is loaded on a cargo plane.

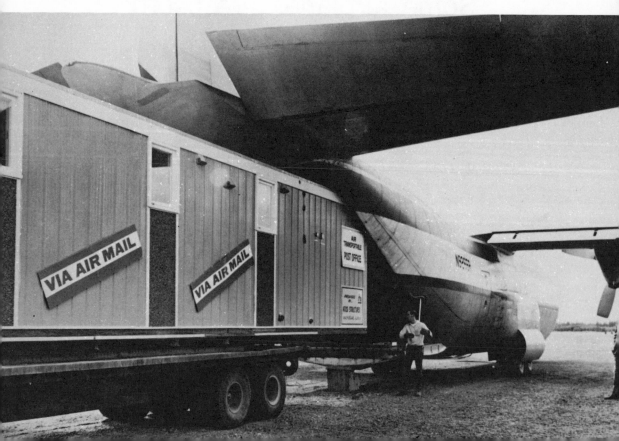

Some airplanes are used to put out forest fires. They can drop a lot of water on a fire from the air.

Some airplanes are used to help farmers.

Airplanes also move the mail. Jets can get the mail across the country in just a few hours. A truck or a train would take much longer.

AIRPORTS

Airplanes take off and land at an airport. The most important part of the airport is the runway. A runway is like a long, smooth street. It has lights down both sides. Then the pilot can see the runway at night.

Some small airplanes
can land and take off on a
dirt road or a farm field.
They don't need a lot of
room. But all large
airplanes must have long
runways. They must build
up speed to take off. They
must have more room to
stop when they land.

THE PILOT
OF AN AIRPLANE

The person who flies an
airplane is called the pilot.
A pilot has many things to
think about. Being a pilot
is not an easy job.

A pilot has to steer the airplane. He must make sure the airplane's engines are running right. He uses a radio to talk to airport workers and to other pilots. A pilot must know a lot about the weather.

Many large airliners have a second pilot. The second pilot is called a copilot. The copilot helps keep watch on all the instruments. He helps do all the other jobs a pilot has to do.

HOW THE
AIRPLANE IS RUN

The pilot sits in the front of an airplane. This is called the cockpit.

A pilot uses a steering yoke or control stick to fly the airplane. To make a left turn, the pilot turns the yoke to the left. To turn right, he turns the steering yoke to the right. When the pilot pulls back on the yoke, the airplane goes up. When he pushes forward on the yoke, the airplane goes down.

Flight instruments tell the pilot many important things.

- How fast the airplane is flying (Air-speed indicator)

- How high the airplane is flying (Altimeter)

- What direction the airplane is flying (Compass)

- How the engines are running (Engine gauges)

Instruments are important for a pilot flying at night or in thick clouds. Using instruments, the pilot can fly the airplane without seeing outside it.

Airplanes carry both packages and people.

The Space Shuttle, *Enterprise*, is an aircraft that can carry people and goods into space. Its sister ship, the *Columbia*, made its first successful space flight in 1981.

Today , airplanes are very important. They're fast and safe. They help us do many things.

WORDS YOU SHOULD KNOW

airliner (AIR • ly • ner) — an airplane which carries people

bomber (BAHM • er) — an airplane which carries bombs

cockpit (KAHK • pit) — the part of an airplane where the pilot sits

control stick (kun • TROHL stik) — the part of an airplane which is used to steer it

copilot (KOH • py • lit) — the second pilot of an airplane

engine (EN • jin) — a machine that uses energy to make something run or move; motor

experimental (eks • PEER • uh • MEN • til) — new and still being tested

fighter (FY • ter) — small airplane used in battle

flap — move up and down

flight (FLYT) — to fly; an airplane trip

giant (JY • ent) — very, very big

glider (GLY • der) — an airplane without an engine

glue (GLEW) — a liquid used to stick things together

goggles (GOG • uhls) — special glasses used to cover and protect the eyes

helicopter (HEL • ih • kop • ter) — an aircraft without wings

important (im • POHR • tunt) — having great value

instead (in • STED) — in place of; rather than

instrument (IN • struh • ment) — something used to show information

jet — an airplane with a special engine and no propeller

large — big

military (MIL • uh • tayr • ee) — having to do with soldiers and fighting

passenger (PASS • in • jer) — a person who travels in an airplane

pilot (PY • lit) — the person who operates an airplane

power — energy

private (PRY • vit)—owned by a person or a group; not public

propeller (pruh • PELL • er)—something that has blades which spin when attached to a motor

runway—land on which an airplane takes off and lands

rush—to go fast; quick

soar (SOHR)—to fly

solar-powered (SOH • ler POW • erd)—to run with power gotten from the sun's light

sound barrier (SOWND BEHR • ee • uhr)—an imaginary point where airplanes travel faster than sound

speed—to move quickly

sport—something done for fun

steer—to guide

super sonic (SOO • per SOHN • ik)—faster than the speed of sound

tow (TOE)—to pull

vertical (VER • tih • kul)—straight up and down

weigh (WAY)—to find out how heavy something is

yoke—a lever that moves outside parts of an airplane to make the plane go up and down

INDEX

About the Author

David Petersen started his flying career in the military service. He served in the Orient and on aircraft carriers in the Pacific. Upon leaving the service he joined the staff of a touring-motorcycle magazine, where he became managing editor. David recently moved to Durango, Colorado. He makes his living as a free-lance writer and photographer, and spends his spare time hiking and camping in the mountains. He also holds a commercial helicopter pilot's license.

A New True Book

DINOSAURS

By Mary Lou Clark

This "true book" was prepared
under the direction of
Illa Podendorf,
formerly with the Laboratory School,
University of Chicago

 CHILDRENS PRESS, CHICAGO

Plesiosaurus

PHOTO CREDITS
Richard Wahl—4,6,7,8,9,10,13,14,17,18,19,20,22,23,26,30,31,32,34,36,37
Field Museum of Natural History, Chicago—2,28
James P. Rowan—cover, 24 (2 photos), 44 (top)
Reinhard Brucker—39
National Museum of Natural History, Smithsonian Institution—40 (top), 44 (bottom)
Connecticut Department of Economic Development—40 (bottom)
U.S. Department of Interior, National Park Service: Dinosaur National Monument—43
Cover—Life-size model of Triceratops at the Smithsonian Institution, Washington D.C.

Library of Congress Cataloging in Publication Data
   Clark, Mary Lou.
   Dinosaurs.
   (A New True book)
   Previously published as: The true book of dinosaurs.
1955.
   SUMMARY: Briefly describes a number of different
dinosaurs, what came before and after them, why they
disappeared, and how we have learned about them.
   1.   Dinosaurs—Juvenile literature.   [1.   Dinosaurs]
I.   Title.
QE862.D5C54   1981   567.9′1   81-7750
ISBN 0-516-01612-1   AACR2

TABLE OF CONTENTS

BRONTOSAURUS

TYRANNOSAURUS
REX

TRICERATOPS

STEGOSAURUS

CORYTHOSAURUS

DIPLODOCUS

MODERN HORSE

DINOSAURS

The word dinosaur
means "Terrible Lizard."
Years and years ago,
more than you can count,
these great animals lived
on the earth.
There were no people
then.

BRONTOSAURUS

"Thunder Lizard" was as big as ten elephants. It was a plant eater.

Thunder Lizard has another name— Brontosaurus. Brontosaurus means Thunder Lizard.

Some of the time,
Thunder Lizards stood in
the water. They ate the
plants that grew there. The
water helped the Thunder
Lizards hold up their heavy
bodies.

7

"Longest Lizard" looked
a great deal like Thunder
Lizard. It was a plant
eater, too.

Can you imagine how
big it was?

DIPLODOCUS

Measure a string eighty times as long as this picture. This is how big Longest Lizard was.

STEGOSAURUS

"Armored Lizard" lived on land. It was a plant eater.

Armored Lizard had hard plates of bone along its back. These plates of bone helped protect it from meat eaters.

There was a "Leaping Lizard." It lived on land. It was a meat eater.

ALLOSAURUS

ALLOSAURUS
FIGHTING
BRONTOSAURUS

The meat eaters were
enemies of the plant
eaters.

14

The meat eaters went
after the Thunder Lizards
when they came out of the
water.

Thunder Lizards were too
heavy to run away. They
had only their tails and
teeth to fight with.

Often they lost to the
meat eaters.

Millions and millions of years went by. Slowly changes took place.

The first of the dinosaurs disappeared from the earth. But other dinosaurs appeared.

"Tyrant King" was the most fierce of all. Tyrant King was a meat eater. He had big jaws and sharp teeth.

TYRANNOSAURUS REX

CORYTHOSAURUS

"Duck-billed Lizard" had
a mouth shaped like a
duck's. It had many rows
of teeth.

PROTOCERATOPS

One of the smaller plant-eating dinosaurs had a sharp beak.

It had a shield-shaped skull bone at the back of its head, too.

Its beak, teeth, and skull helped protect it from the meat-eating dinosaurs.

TRICERATOPS

"Three-horned Face" had three horns. It had a shield-shaped bone in back of its head. Horn-faced lizards were plant eaters. They used their horns to fight off the fierce Tyrant King.

PLESIOSAURUS

At the time of the
dinosaurs, big lizard-like
animals lived in the sea.
There were "Near
Lizards" with long necks.
There were "Fish
Lizards" that were more
like fish.

ICHTHYOSAUR

American Alligator

Iguana

Millions and millions of years went by. The earth changed. The weather changed. The big dinosaurs did not change fast enough. They died.

Now there are no dinosaurs. But there are animals living today that belong to the same group of animals as the dinosaurs. Some reptiles are like dinosaurs.

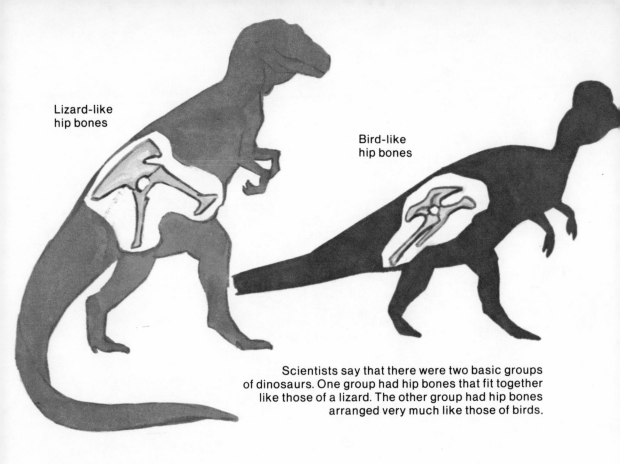

Lizard-like
hip bones

Bird-like
hip bones

Scientists say that there were two basic groups
of dinosaurs. One group had hip bones that fit together
like those of a lizard. The other group had hip bones
arranged very much like those of birds.

Many birds are like other
dinosaurs, especially the
small meat eaters.
Today many scientists
think dinosaurs were
closest to the bird family.

WHAT CAME BEFORE THE DINOSAURS ?

Before there were dinosaurs, there were many other kinds of animals. Some lived in the sea. Some lived on land.

The very first animals
lived in the sea. They were
small. Many of them had
shells.

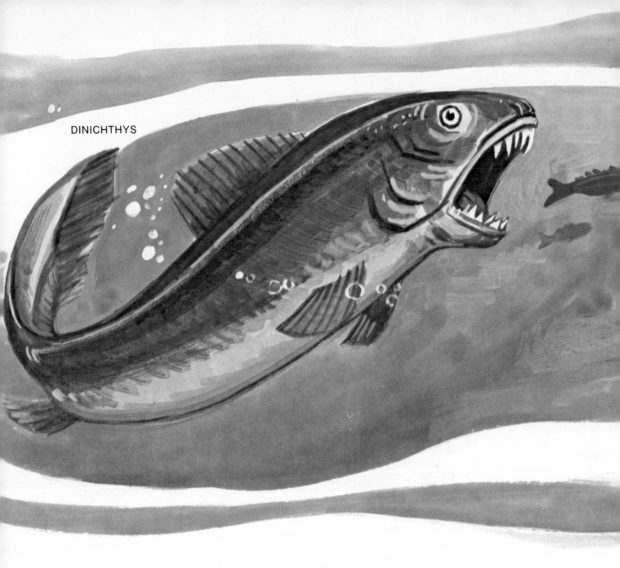

DINICHTHYS

Later there were fish.
One of the biggest of
these was the "Terrible
Fish."

30

ERYOPS

"Drawn-out Face" was
one of the first animals to
walk on land. It had
smooth skin. It could live
in water and on land.

DIMETRODON

Many years before the dinosaurs appeared there was a "Sail-Back" animal that lived on land.

EARLY
MAMMALS

The dinosaurs laid eggs. They often left the eggs to hatch, just as some reptiles do today.

Before the dinosaurs disappeared, there were some small animals called mammals. Mammals are animals that give birth to their young. They feed their young milk. Sometimes mammals have to fight to keep their young safe.

MAMMOTH

MASTODON

SABER-TOOTHED TIGER

WHAT CAME AFTER THE DINOSAURS ?

After all the dinosaurs were gone there were large mammals on the earth. Now, some of these are gone, too.

FOSSILS:
STORIES IN STONE

If there were no people in the world, how do we know about these animals of long ago?

Many animals have left a story. The story is found in the layers of rock of the earth.

Digging for dinosaur bones in Utah.

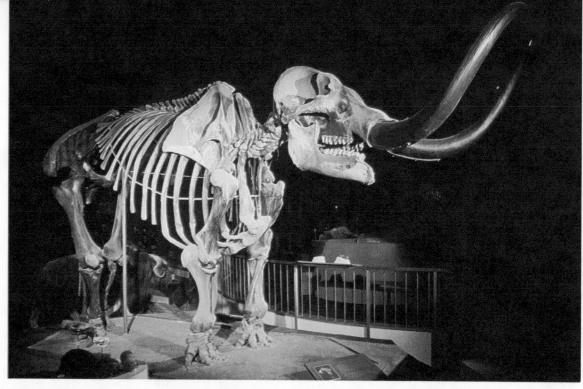

This North American mastodon lived from coast to coast from Alaska to Mexico.

Dinosaur footprints in Connecticut

Animals died and left their bones. They left their footprints. Many of these bones and footprints have been found. They had been changed to stone. They are called fossils.

People study the fossils. A rock with a fossil in it may be sent to a museum. In the museum the fossils are set up so that many people can see them.

Fossils tell us about the size of the dinosaurs. They tell us what dinosaurs probably ate.

Scientist digs out dinosaur bones in Dinosaur National Monument.

Camarasaurus

Fossil of a saber-toothed tiger found in California

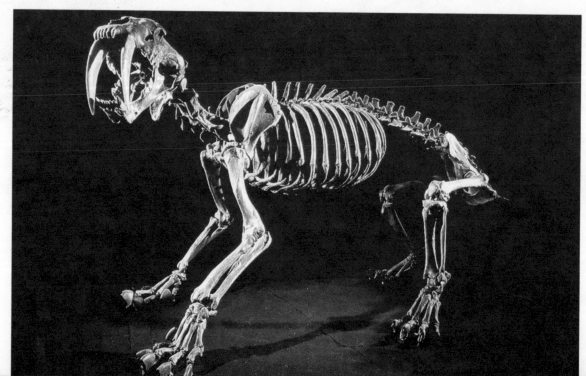

There is still much of the story to be found out. Dinosaurs are only a small part of a much bigger story, the story of our earth and how it changed.

Someday you will want to read more of the story that fossils tell.

WORDS YOU SHOULD KNOW

appear (uh•PEER)—to be seen

armoured (ARE•merrd)—covered with a heavy covering like shells or plates

beak (BEEK)—bill; the hard parts of a mouth

dinosaur (DY•nuh•sore)—a kind of animal that lived long ago

disappear (dis•uh•PEER)—not be seen; vanish

duck-billed (DUK•billd)—shaped with a broad, flat bill like a duck's

earth (ERTH)—our world; the planet on which we live

enemy (EN•uh•mee)—not a friend

especially (es•PESH•uh•lee)—in a special way; more than usually

fierce (FEERSS)—dangerous; wild; mean

fossil (FOSS•ill)—the remains of plants and animals that lived long ago

great (GRAYT)—big; very large

heavy (HEV•ee)—having much weight

horn—hard, pointed growth on some animals' heads

jaw—the upper and lower parts of the mouth

layer—a thickness

leaping (LEE•ping)—jumping

lizard (LIZ•erd)—an animal with four legs, a tail, and a body covered with scales; a reptile

mammal (MAM•ihl)—an animal covered with hair or fur

measure(MEH•zher)—to figure the size of something

museum (myu•ZEE•um)—a building for keeping and showing interesting and valuable things

plate—a hard, bony covering of an animal

probably (PROB • ub • lee)—likely to happen

protect (proh • TEKT)—to keep safe; guard

reptile (REP • tyl)—a cold-blooded animal with a backbone and covered with scales or plates

row—placed in a line

sail-backed (SAYL • bakd)—shaped like a sail

sea (SEE)—a body of salt water

sharp—pointed

shell—hard outer covering of some animals

shield-shaped (SHEELD-shaypd)—in the shape of a shield— usually three-sided

smooth—not rough; even

terrible (TAIR • ih • buhl)—not pleasant; fearful; bad

thunder (THUN • der)—loud noise

tyrant (TY • rent)—cruel; not nice

INDEX

About the Author

Mary Lou Clark earned her Master of Science degree at the University of Pittsburgh and her Ph.D. degree at San Diego State University. She has taught high school chemistry and physics and once hosted a TV science show for children. Married and the mother of four children, Mrs. Clark has written numerous magazine articles and stories both for juvenile and adult readers.